We Slept Here

We Slept Here

Sierra DeMulder

Button Poetry / Exploding Pinecone Press
Minneapolis, Minnesota
2015

Published by Button Poetry / Exploding Pinecone Press
Minneapolis, MN 55403

http://buttonpoetry.com

Cover Design: Doug Paul Case || dougpaulcase@gmail.com

ISBN 978-0-9896415-8-6

This book is dedicated to you—who I was meant to find, who I loved so fiercely once.

TABLE OF CONTENTS

...the landscape/ after cruelty which is, of course, a garden
—Richard Siken, "Snow and Dirty Rain"

AND IF I AM TO FORGIVE YOU

Who am I

if I am not
the aftertaste

of abuse?

The offspring
of your temper

and your fat

white pills?
I don't know

what will be left

of me if I dump
the curdled milk

down the drain.

Sometimes I just
like to look at it,

open the fridge

and let the cold
sharpen my skin.

Be someone

who bought
milk once.

A poet told me

to write about
you. *Write it*

out, honey.

As if you were
a fever or

a horse to break.

As if you don't
already show up,

uninvited,

unbeckoned,
into every poem.

Your hand

guides my wrist
as I write this,

even now.

MY SISTER REMEMBERS

the sharp, feral way our father spoke

      to the maker of his children.

How his whole face became a mouth.

      How he hissed and spat and

huffed like a hell engine. How our

      mother became more chair

than voice, her whole body an opening.

      An echo chamber. How he

said words we did not know but knew

      were bad and would repeat

like gaudy hyenas to our cousins.

      How we too became animals.

How she went limp as a snipped lily,

      a wax doll going soft next to

the stove. It is not that my father yelled

and it is not that my mother

received his yelling. It is that we

remember them like this,

in tandem, bound forever with ribbon,

a call and response. It is that

in our minds, one does not exist

without the other.

A STUDY OF FORGIVENESS AS A CHILD

She plays in the yard and waves
at all the strangers. She loves juice
and drinks it until it forms a river

down the front of her belly, until
a pink stain floats above her lip.
She is always naked the way adults

can never be. Grown folk undress
in the dark, slide the stocking
of the day off but never the shame.

Forgiveness is too young to think
nakedness is different. She dances
in the sprinkler, thumping her chest

like a bible and howling like a puppy
storm. We adults are afraid of what
the world could do with her soft pelt.

Her openness. How we would gut
her honesty, not like a buck but like
an angelfish. Trophy it on our mantel.

When we catch her spoon-feeding
a stranger or letting that man sip
invisible tea from her cupped hands,

we drag her inside by the wrist,
scold her for being so damn gullible.
Hoard her away at the first sign of rain.

WHEN I SHOULD HAVE LEFT YOU

When we stopped fucking in bed.
    Instead, hunched over like the sick
    on the side of the couch, the pool table,
    the front seat of your Cadillac.
    It was no longer the passionate
    lovemaking of the newly obsessed
    attempting to crawl into each other's skin—
    more the way a cat will play with
    a sparrow long after it is dead.

When I accidentally coughed up
    my tongue at the dinner table.
    Out it fell like a piece of veal
    on the mashed potatoes. I hardly
    recognized it, I swallowed it so long ago.

When I realized I felt most in love with you
    when I was high, after you shared
    those pills with me, the chalky marbles
    prescribed to the terminally ill
    that made everything soft and slow.
    Perhaps this was your gift to me.
    Perhaps you knew all along—
    like a surgeon placing the plastic mask
    over my mouth, counting back from twenty—
    that this was going to hurt.

I REMEMBER

The dull thump of a blue jay flying into our window.

The exact number of times the screen door bounced
after my mother, a shapeless color, ran outside.

The dirty dishes, the act of cleaning away what's
left, in the sink next to the featherless chicken
and the empty empty empty bottles.

The smothered sound of shouting behind a door.

How we justified my father's anger—*he had
a long day. It's hot outside. It's not like he hit her.*

Nights spent sliding the screen door open
as soft and quiet as milk sitting in a glass.

A skinned deer on our front porch, a wind chime
of muscle, and the buck knife soaking in the bathtub.

My father's tears, foreign ornaments, startling as
the baby blue jays we found under the porch.

INTO THE DARK

He used to break his Ambien between thumb
and forefinger as if pinching the head off
a tick. Then, like a good mama bird, drop it

into my chirping mouth. I liked these pills,
this maternal ritual. In a way, it was gentle.
In a way, he gave me permission to leave,

slip out of my body to a world in which
he could not follow. Sometimes I would try
to resist—draw wildly in an old sketchbook

until the last drop of gasoline was siphoned
from the tank and I would sputter into dark.
Once, he found me on the couch, ignoring

the heavy awning of sleep, penciling
a flowered woman unlocking her mouth.
What a pretty picture, darling. The rope

slipping from my fingers. *What a pity,*
fix her, darling. The lantern sinking into
the lake. *What a gritty elixir, starling.*

When I woke, the book was still open in
my lap. The woman's eyes were scratched out.
Her mouth stuffed with a sail. *Leave. Leave!*

1

2

During the worst of it, during the blur of Christmas-turned-
New-Year's-turned-a-dull-January, when we lived in his
hometown, where there were only trees and fields and empty
roads, where I was brought and kept without a car or a bicycle
or a damn sled to leave on, where the closest neighbor was his
grandfather, where we learned the worst of our love, where I
wasn't allowed to use my phone or check my email, where I
could reply but only if he was in the room, only if he was the one
responding, where my hair started to fall out, where my period
was late, where it came, sudden and dark, down my leg in his
kitchen, where I deleted the worried texts from my friends
while he slept, where one friend made for me a cypher through
which we could speak, *1 = ARE YOU OKAY?, 2 = YES, 3 = NO*,
where he wouldn't look at me for hours, where I was so sure that
I was disgusting, boiled down to bone, in my marrow, I
deserved this, *1*, when he made me fuck in the car, in the front
seat, the moving car while he drove, *2*, when he had a bad day, *2*,
when he had a good day, *2*, when he would drink all the right
drinks and take the right pills that would make him so sweet,
when he was so sweet and honeysuckle sorry, when he turned
back into a wolf, when I loved him this whole time.

A STUDY OF FORGIVENESS AS A PIÑATA

It is definitely an animal, but nobody can tell
which kind. Half donkey, half rodeo clown.

Part cow, part hummingbird. People

only care what's inside, and how eventually
it will be violently drawn out—the wild

staggers of the blindfolded, how the body

acts as a volume knob: the closer the swing,
the louder the shrieks. That satisfying thud,

aluminum against papier-mâché, dull

and electric. In these years after you, I too
have thrashed in the dark, have swung madly

at sounds, have prayed for impact, or at least

purpose. I confess I have noosed your memory,
waved my bat like a shameful finger, waited

beneath it, ready to collect my lump of closure.

Thump. *I forgive you.* Thump. *I forgive you.*
Thump. Thump. Thump. Thump.

Nothing ever falls out.

KNOCK KNOCK

who's there?

drug addict.

no, he is not.

who's there?

night out with yr man

night out with
my man who?

needs a little kick, he says,
snagged some faceless
pills off a stranger, he says,

take one & I

take one.

knock knock?

who's there?

black out.
          black out who
not yet, silly.   *not yet, stupid.*
we gotta get drunk first.
we gotta stagger back

          to the hotel, undress,
          we are making
          desperate love, bodies
          stumbling down the ally
          of ourselves and

you drop
          mid fuck

heavy as a carcass
          might as well have been

knock knock

you come to & he

          is getting dressed.
          I wake up & don't
          know where I am

or how long you've been

          asleep or why he is looking
          at me like that

knock knock

you just passed out

he is angry.

while we were fucking.

what did you expect him to do

just sit around
and watch you sleep?

no wait, please,
I don't know
what's wrong with

please

help

who's there?

he left me left me.
I am a heavy coat

of paint. the room spins.

the paint

fills my head.
my fingers

cotton balls. my eyelids

pockets of

stones. I sink,

drown.

knock knock sleepy head

who's there?

wake up.

wake up who?

not yr legs. not
for a while. the side effects are
worst in the morning.

I crawl to the shower

vomit under the hot rain.

he left me he left me

you say again and again

I am a ship with no
helm, a graveyard

with no dirt.

crows fill my stomach.

I dial his number.

where are you?

no where

knock knock

        what.

the joke is

you stay for another
six months.

the joke is

        this is not enough

        to make me
        leave.

A STUDY OF FORGIVENESS
AS A ONE-NIGHT STAND

She wants to say it without thinking.

She wants to touch it without truly
knowing who she is touching—

the stranger, the friend, the unimpressive

barista who wants to show her
his tapestry collection. Just let her

give it without giving it. Let her say

the words without opening her mouth.
I forgive you   I forgive you she wants

the quick high, the counterfeit, the *oh*

god, the false idol. She wants to pray
without believing. She wants to give you

her body without being in the room.

O HOLY

How do you describe the feeling
of waking up? Darkness, and then,
not. Consciousness becomes the slow
drawing of a bath. My mind begins to fill.
My senses trickle back from blackness.
Still dark, but lighter like drying paint.
I become aware of my surroundings
shadow by shadow: the bed, the pillows,
the sheets, the hands. Trees thrash
against my hips, the window, but strange,
there is no storm. Still shadows. Something
is pushing, knocking at my body. How
do you describe penetration? I become aware
of the sliding, archaic thrust, the filling
of what is bottomless. Consciousness
now spills over the lip of the tub
and I am drowning. Who are you?
I am awake, my body screams, awake,
but my mouth does not remember itself.
Who are you? Nothing but shadow
falls from my mouth. For what seems
like a year, I do not know who is inside me.
Here is the light bulb. Here is the gasp of air.
It's you, you, you, my lover. O thank god.
O holy mistake. I realize that it is you
and that I am safe and I cry fat, instant tears.
You pull out of me, confused, angry
we stopped. I explain I was dreaming.
I explain people wake up entangled

all the time, I just didn't know who
I was tied to, didn't know who was knocking
at the door of me. And see, even though
we will still sleep beside each other
for six more weeks, this is the exact
moment you lose me: I tell you
I thought I was being raped
and you ask me who I was dreaming of.
O holy abuser. O green-eyed wolf.
You say I moaned like a ghost
in my sleep, panted, pushed against
you like a strung-back bow. You say
I must want it from someone else.
To this day, this is what I think of
when I think of you.

A STUDY OF FORGIVENESS
AS A PROCESS OR A SOCIOPATH

Except

this time is not about forgiveness.

Instead, how sometimes

I fantasize about actually physically

hurting you. I have dreamt

of kicking you, pulling out slivers

of your hair, as if violence

is the patron saint of healing—cause

damage to repair damage.

Anger lives so loud in the body.

The dirtiest of my heart

enjoys picturing you alone. Wilted.

Soaking in a bathtub

of nails, swallowing one for each

cruelty against me. And

wouldn't that be just? Wouldn't

that be so righteous?

Sometimes I think it would be

easier to forgive you

if you weren't so damn unscarred.

AND IF I DO NOT FORGIVE HIM

I have found an identity in its decoration.
A profession in its preening. I polish it
with sequined spit. Dress it in gowns
skinned from his brokenness. Prance

on it like a bear rug. My suffering:
the artist's fodder, the cave I map
endlessly. Lucky that his fault is so
bountiful, a swollen cornucopia. I am fat

off his wrong-doings. I am afraid I will
be like this forever. I write *I forgive you*
onto the paper. Again and again. Until
the pen droughts. Until the page is no longer

a page but a river. A lake. I write over
the surface like a Jesus or a water bug.
I write until the letters do not form letters.
Until the paper is wet soil, or essentially

a tree again. He hangs from its branches.
Not hanged. Not a wind chime. He is no
singer. He is reaching for his ax. There is
a throne in the room where all mercy is made,

and for now, I can sit on it. For now, he can't
reach me up here. I fold the paper over itself
like a building collapsing. Make it as small
as a tongue. I am told I should give it to him.

I am told that forgiveness is a knife with no
handle, not meant to be held, not built
to be a prisoner. But why, dear reader,
would I give my only weapon away?

ON ADMITTING YOU ARE AN ABUSE SURVIVOR

It will not happen the first time

you forgive him. Or the second.
Or the third. It will not happen

the fourth time you break down

in public. A wine glass shatters
at a dinner party and you leave

without saying goodbye. A car

door slammed across the empty
parking lot becomes the animal

urge to call him. It will not happen

even as you write *this* poem—
when you finally claim what

happened to you as if it was a child

you abandoned when you were
too young to know better. You still

can't bring yourself to call it

by name. Are you afraid of how
much it looks like you? How it has

his mouth but *your* eyes. Say it:

I am an abuse survivor. Abuse
survivor. Tell everyone how wrong

your heart was. Share all the horrible

things he did and then tell them
how even now, you are not sure

you wouldn't go back—if only

to say *I'm sorry* one last time.

A STUDY OF FORGIVENESS
AS AN OLD WOMAN

Her back droops over itself

like the handle of an umbrella.
Her feet resemble ginger root,

knobby and dry. She walks

for hours every day with him
papoosed to her back like

a tumor slow-dancing with

her spine. Each day, she picks
wildflowers; braids me a tiara

from tickseed and baby's breath,

crowns me Queen of the Fester.
I want to rest, she begs,

you need to let it go. Again

and again, I send her back
to the road: *Come home*

when he is different, I say.

Come back when you have
found a better breed of me.

YOUR BEST

No matter where you are in life, no matter what you've contributed to creating...you are always doing the best you can with the understanding and awareness and knowledge that you have.
　　　　— Louise L. Hay

And if this was your finest

　　　　performance—no dress rehearsal,
no amputated second act—
　　　　no longer would I grieve

　　　　your potential. No longer
would I wait up for the return
　　　　of your soldiered goodness.

At first, I imagined addiction

　　　　as your finest suit, hung in
the closet, ironed in the dark.
　　　　Now I see you had

　　　　no other option, not even
your own skin, no summer
　　　　jacket or wool coat, only this.

The fine china of your temper,

　　　　the creased linens, the dirtiest
looks I had assumed were
　　　　brought out only for the most

dazzling of dinner parties.
It was never a choice. There was
    no other way for you to love me.

I knew no other way to be loved.

ON ADMITTING YOU ARE AN ABUSE SURVIVOR

It will happen when you try,

so foolishly, to love another:
this doe-eyed heart you found

in the garden. He is soft

and loud, but only when he is
singing, only when he is laughing.

You catch yourself staring

at his teeth, his mouth, searching
for that retractable silence.

Each night, you will try so hard

to touch his face. Your fingers
will shake. You will be crying

and you will not know why

and it's not his fault. It's not his fault
he is an un-swung axe.

STILL

He shows up sometimes
when I am making love
or cleaning the bathroom

or thinking about the way
time is a pendant sliding
on a chain. Out of the blue

smoke of my happiness,
he will appear, and he will
not fill me with fear like

he used to and he will not
name me soundless like
he used to. Instead, I just

stare, as gently as I can,
at his gauntness. True,
I did misplace myself.

True, he did become
a forest that swallowed
and swallowed but he was

the lost one. Now, when
he comes back to me, he
demands what I recognize

as pity. In my dreams,
he is old, thick with regret,
filled with a thousand

voices but ashamed of all
of them. In my dreams,
he is a child. A golden

little boy. He is always
crying. He knows he has to
do this all over again.

AFTER GOOGLING AFFIRMATIONS FOR ABUSE SURVIVORS

You have a fundamental right to a nurturing
      environment. Oh, what a home I have
      built in my skull. What a dark, savage
      forest. There is no furniture, no artisan
      humanity. No gentle place to undress
      my own thoughts.

You are a valuable human. I think about death
      too often. I eat peanut butter with my
      fingers. I pee in the shower. I am
      a mouthful. Not a swallow. Not a bird
      or a name gone sour in his mouth.

If you allow yourself to be mistreated, you are
      teaching that it is okay for others to
      abuse you. And look at this shining
      curriculum! The lessons I have been
      prepping for months! Now, class,
      take out your inner child. Tell her
      she is so selfish. Tell her she shouldn't
      have eaten the last of the truffles.
      Tell her to take a good long look
      at love: her father gripping the throat
      of the payphone.

You cannot assume responsibility or accept
      blame for any abusive behavior. I am
      so sorry so sorry sorry so sorry he is

so sorry sorry sorry so so sorry again
and again the conductor lifts her baton
and the musicians tilt their horns and
the song begins again.

You do not have to feel guilty for allowing others
to take care of themselves. But what
do I do with all this leftover love?
My hands were built for crawling on.
How do I write myself gently? How
do I not worship the shipwreck that
stranded me here?

You are not a failure or less of a person because
you make mistakes. I am not a failure
or less of a person because I make
mistakes. I write this until my hand
becomes a beggar. I write this until
the words no longer sound like words,
only sounds, and I can believe them now.

Your higher power is transforming your brokenness
and gently carrying you from darkness
into light. I believe in gentleness. Lord,
I believe in light. I am my own higher
power. I will carry myself out.

RELEASE IT

You are not the first to domesticate it.
Your shame: pretty as a house pet.
You bathe it nightly, comb its matted
carpet. When will you stop letting it

sleep in your bed? Some part of it
comforts you—that dank heaviness
curled at your feet like a birds nest
of forks. When will you put it down?

End its reign, its gnarled suckling
of your last good teat? You, on
your knees, still. You, crawling out
of that man's mouth, still. Let go

of the fact that you were the other
woman, once, twice. Lust spent like
inheritance does not define you.
Let go of being made of want: *yes,*

*I ate all six macaroons on the sparkling
streets of Budapest that night. I saved
none for you.* Sweetheart, shame has
been bound in your basement too long.

Release it. Your floorboards shudder
at the thought of your belly, smooth
as an apple, kissing flat against it.
Release it. Your hands are not

as small as they used to be. Get up.
This is not who you are anymore.
Worth is not a well to be poisoned.
It is not a tumbler being filled or

drank from by some audacious god,
nor a monthly allowance we get
when we are not not beautiful.
Drive to the ocean. No, drive to

the Redwoods. Drive to whatever
landmark most reminds you that
becoming is a slow glory and leave
your shame. It will not follow you home.

UNINHABITABLE

My father still lives in the house he built
for my mother. He calls himself a bachelor,

not a hoarder, but you can measure how long
she's been gone using the piles of expired

mail, the dishes, the sun-stained photos framed
in dust. When he speaks of his recovery,

he lowers his voice, even though he lives alone
and it's just us at his cluttered kitchen table.

He tells me he isn't ashamed of what he did
or where he has been or what he put my mother

through, but I think he means that he does
not allow himself the luxury of forgetting.

      :::

I am writing about you again today and
I wonder, why dig up our sad corpse?

Why put the spleen back, a spoiled balloon,
already burst, but here I am huffing life back

into it. Nursing our fruitless love. Sometimes,
I still can't believe it. That you happened

and I happened and this was the best we could
do. Our nest of rubbish, our flowerless

garden—we slept here. Made love among
the bottles caps and ants and mold.

:::

My father told me he still imagines getting back
together with my mother, maybe someday, after

her new husband dies. I think he means he started
to build a house and left it unfinished. What is it about

this family that draws us back to the uninhabitable?
That compels us to make a bed where there isn't one.

AND IF I AM TO FORGIVE MYSELF

I am not afraid that he will happen
again, but that I inevitably will.
My biggest fear is the belief that
I am and always will be rotten, right
down to my blueprints, unworthy
of love, even one as sickly as this.
To forgive oneself is not only to
admit fault, to recognize what land
you tilled to grow here, but to
also say (and somehow believe)
I did not deserve this. Neither did he.

I have always imagined forgiveness
as a garden. A serene landscape
with perfect paths and soft lighting,
not a leaf out of place. But forgiveness
cannot merely be an assembly of lovely
things or the act of meandering pass.
It must be the mud also. It must be
the weeds and the mosquitos and
the hundreds of miles it took you to
walk there. It has to be showing up,
finally, sweaty and sore, only to realize
you went to the wrong fucking garden.

So here's to our blistered feet. Here's
to my whimpering knees, your weary
shoulders. Here is the foreclosure
of my shame and here is to our
brokenness. Look at us being so

43

damn human: yes, it happened,
yes, it was not our most graceful
unfolding, and yes, we were both
so present the whole time.

ACKNOWLEDGMENTS

This book would not exist without the talent and patience of Michael Mlekoday, Neil Hilborn, Sam Cook, Rya DeMulder, and Brian Lenz.

No one should live in fear of the person they love. If you have or are experiencing any form of abuse, please know you are not alone and you are not responsible for their behavior. No matter what you did, you do not deserve this. In addition to personal and professional support, I found the following resources helpful:

You Can Heal Your Life
by Louise Hay

Live Through This: On Creativity and Self-Destruction
edited by Sabrina Chapadjiev

All About Love: New Visions
by bell hooks

"Tailor" by Anaïs Mitchell

"Hood" by Perfume Genius

"Bulletproof" by La Roux

Milano cookies

RESOURCES

The National Domestic Violence Hotline
1-800-799-7233 (SAFE)
www.ndvh.org

National Dating Abuse Helpline
1-866-331-9474
www.loveisrespect.org

National Sexual Assault Hotline
1-800-656-4673 (HOPE)
www.rainn.org

National Suicide Prevention Lifeline
1-800-273-8255 (TALK)
www.suicidepreventionlifeline.org

National Teen Dating Abuse Helpline
1-866-331-9474
www.loveisrespect.org

Casa de Esperanza
1-651-772-1611
www.casadeesperanza.org

The National Immigrant Women's Advocacy Project
1-202-274-4457
www.niwap.org

National Indigenous Women's Resource Center
855-649-7299
www.niwrc.org

Asian and Pacific Islander Institute on Domestic Violence
1-415-954-9988
www.apiidv.org

Institute on Domestic Violence in the African American Community
1-877-643-8222
www.idvaac.org

GLBTQ Domestic Violence Project
1-800-832-1901
www.glbtqdvp.org

National Organization for Men Against Sexism (NOMAS)
1-720-466-3882
www.nomas.org

National Human Trafficking Resource Center
1-888-373-7888
www.traffickingresourcecenter.org

Legal Momentum
1-212-925-6635
www.legalmomentum.org

WomensLaw.org
www.womenslaw.org

Signs of Abusive Relationships
www.helpguide.org/articles/abuse/domestic-violence-and-abuse.htm

ABOUT THE AUTHOR

Sierra DeMulder is an internationally touring performance poet and educator, a two-time National Poetry Slam champion, and the author of two books (*The Bones Below* and *New Shoes on a Dead Horse*, Write Bloody Publishing). She is the curriculum director of the Gustavus Adolphus College Institute of Spoken Word and Poetry Slam, an annual writing summer camp for high school students, and one of the founders of Button Poetry, the largest digital distributor of spoken word media in the world. Her third full-length collection, *Today Means Amen*, will be published by Andrews McMeel Publishing in spring of 2016. Sierra lives in Minneapolis with her dog, Fidelis.

OTHER BOOKS BY BUTTON POETRY

Aziza Barnes, *me Aunt Jemima and the nailgun.*

J. Scott Brownlee, *Highway or Belief*

Sam Sax, *A Guide to Undressing Your Monsters*

Nate Marshall, *Blood Percussion*

Mahogany L. Browne, *smudge*

Neil Hilborn, *Our Numbered Days*

Available at buttonpoetry.com/shop